To

_____

From

_____

Date

_____

Daily Inspirations of Blessings

© 2007 Christian Art Gifts, RSA
            Christian Art Gifts Inc., IL, USA

Designed by Christian Art Gifts

Unless otherwise indicated Scripture quotations are taken from the *Holy Bible*, New International Version® NIV®. Copyright © 1973, 1978, 1984 by International Bible Society. Used by permission of Zondervan Publishing House. All rights reserved.

Scripture quotations marked NLT are taken from the *Holy Bible*, New Living Translation, first edition, copyright © 1996. Used by permission of Tyndale House Publishers, Inc., Carol Stream, Illinois 60188. All rights reserved.

Printed in China

ISBN 978-1-86920-365-8

11 12 13 14 15 16 17 18 19 20 – 23 22 21 20 19 18 17 16 15 14

daily inspirations

of
blessings

Carolyn Larsen

christian
art gifts®

Introduction

❧

Blessings are the encouragements that make life so much more enjoyable. Appreciating the blessings God sprinkles throughout your life helps to get you through the tough times.

Blessings come in many forms and have many faces. Sometimes you may be overwhelmed at the blessings in your life, and other times you may need to stop and remind yourself of them.

Blessings are a reminder that God loves you and that He is paying attention to you and what's going on in your world. Stop, look and appreciate the blessings all around you.

The Blessing of Blessings

There are times for everyone when life is just so constant, so routine. Those are the times when it's easy to get bogged down in the day-in and day-out stuff of just living. You get up in the morning, deal with getting the kids out the door, work all day, run errands, make dinner, help with homework, nag about bath time and bedtime, do some laundry, clean up the house and collapse into bed – only to know that you will do the whole routine over again tomorrow.

Blessings come in the form of interruptions to the routine. It may be a random act of kindness; a hug around the neck from a child; a friend dropping by with coffee; a sudden awareness of the beauty of the creation around you or a momentary lifting of the spiritual curtain to show you how very much God loves you.

Blessings are a blessing. They encourage in the midst of heaviness, bring moments of joy in the midst of the daily occurrences. They make the routine easier to deal with. Thank God for the blessing of blessings.

Blessed is the man who does not walk in the counsel of the wicked or stand in the way of sinners or sit in the seat of mockers. But his delight is in the law of the LORD, and on His law he meditates day and night.

Psalm 1:1-2

Blessed is the man who trusts in the LORD, whose confidence is in Him.

Jeremiah 17:7

Let us not become weary in doing good, for at the proper time we will reap a harvest if we do not give up.

Galatians 6:9

I will pour water on the thirsty land, and streams on the dry ground; I will pour out My Spirit on your offspring, and My blessing on your descendants.

Isaiah 44:3

Blessings crown the head of the righteous, but violence overwhelms the mouth of the wicked.

Proverbs 10:6

The blessing of the LORD brings wealth, and He adds no trouble to it.

Proverbs 10:22

May the God of hope fill you with all joy and peace as you trust in Him, so that you may overflow with hope by the power of the Holy Spirit.

Romans 15:13

Surely You have granted him eternal blessings and made him glad with the joy of Your presence.

Psalm 21:6

The more we count the blessings
we have, the less we
crave the luxuries we haven't.
                    William A. Ward

❧

Dear Father, You are so good to me. You fill
my life with so many wonderful things that,
I must confess, I sometimes take for granted.
Please awaken me to the multitude of bless-
ings You shower down on me every day.

                              Amen.

The Blessing of Guidance

If you've ever been lost in a strange city, or if you're map-challenged, you probably know the frustration of attempting to find your way around. You stumble across one-way or dead-end streets.

Buildings and landmarks begin to all look the same. Every turn seems to take you farther away from your goal. It becomes frightening. You feel hopeless that you will ever find your way.

One of the blessings of knowing God is that your life journey doesn't need to be like a map-challenged journey. A heart that seeks God's direction will be rewarded with guidance from Him because God does have a plan for each of us.

Sometimes it takes effort and certainly patience to discover what that plan is, but if you truly look for it and wait for His guidance, it will come. What a blessing to know you do not need to wander aimlessly through life with no purpose. He has a plan and He will reveal it to you.

"For I know the plans I have for you," declares the LORD, "plans to prosper you and not to harm you, plans to give you hope and a future."

Jeremiah 29:11

In all your ways acknowledge Him, and He will make your paths straight.

Proverbs 3:6

I will instruct you and teach you in the way you should go; I will counsel you and watch over you.

Psalm 32:8

But when He, the Spirit of truth, comes, He will guide you into all truth.

John 16:13

Show me Your ways, O LORD, teach me Your paths; guide me in Your truth and teach me, for You are God my Savior, and my hope is in You all day long.

Psalm 25:4-5

May the Lord direct your hearts into God's love and Christ's perseverance.

2 Thessalonians 3:5

Jesus answered, "I am the way and the truth and the life. No one comes to the Father except through me."

John 14:6

In Your unfailing love You will lead the people You have redeemed. In Your strength You will guide them to Your holy dwelling.

Exodus 15:13

*I was going around in a circle
until Jesus gave me a compass.*
Lynn Langley

❧

*Dear Father, it sometimes feel like I'm going
in circles. I do need Your direction in my life,
daily! Please Father, help me to seek Your direction and then to follow it. Help me to trust
You more and myself less.*

Amen.

The Blessing of Prayer

Conversation helps relationships grow. Over time good conversations help you understand another person. You learn what's important to that person and what his or her dreams are. You can share your own feelings, dreams, concerns and hopes. Conversation is vitally important to getting to know another person. When conversation remains shallow small talk, it's hard to feel that you are really getting to know the other person.

Prayer is a conversation. At times it may feel one-sided, but it really isn't. Prayer is the opportunity to talk with God; to tell Him what's important to you, what's weighing on your heart. It's a chance to share your hopes and dreams. It also presents the opportunity to be silent before God and listen for Him to converse with you.

He will; through your thoughts; through bringing Scripture verses to mind; through the yearnings and feelings in your heart. Prayer is a conversation between you and your God. What a blessing to be able to talk to God in prayer.

If My people, who are called by My name, will humble themselves and pray and seek My face and turn from their wicked ways, then will I hear from heaven and will forgive their sin and will heal their land.

2 Chronicles 7:14

Do not be anxious about anything, but in every-thing, by prayer and petition, with thanksgiving, present your requests to God. And the peace of God, which transcends all understanding, will guard your hearts and your minds in Christ Jesus.

Philippians 4:6-7

The prayer of a righteous man is powerful and ef-fective.

James 5:16

"Therefore I tell you, whatever you ask for in prayer, believe that you have received it, and it will be yours."

Mark 11:24

The LORD is near to all who call on Him, to all who call on Him in truth.

Psalm 145:18

"Ask and it will be given to you; seek and you will find; knock and the door will be opened to you."

Matthew 7:7

Pray continually; give thanks in all circumstances, for this is God's will for you in Christ Jesus.

1 Thessalonians 5:17-18

This is the confidence we have in approaching God: that if we ask anything according to His will, He hears us. And if we know that He hears us – whatever we ask – we know that we have what we asked of Him.

1 John 5:14-15

Prayer is not a substitute for work,
thinking, watching, suffering
or giving; prayer is a support
for all other efforts.

George Buttrick

❧

Dear Father, I know that I often take the
privilege and blessing of being able to pray for
granted. Please forgive me, Father. Help me to
draw on Your mighty power through the gift
of prayer.

Amen.

The Blessing of Forgiveness

What if there was no such thing as forgiveness? What if, when you hurt someone, made a bad choice or disobeyed, that was just it and there was no chance to make it right? What if a relationship was destroyed by your actions and nothing could fix it?

That would make life pretty sad and hopeless, wouldn't it? Carry that thought past the human realm – what if there was no forgiveness from God? There would be no hope of a relationship with Him.

You need not worry about any of this thanks to the blessing of forgiveness. God's forgiveness is our model because it is complete. When we confess and repent of our sins, He forgives us. He will never throw those sins back at us. He forgives and forgets.

That's the model for our relationships. Forgive and forget. It's a blessing to be forgiven and have a relationship restored. It's also a blessing to be the one who does the forgiving. Be as willing to be the forgiver as the one forgiven.

Bear with each other and forgive whatever grievances you may have against one another. Forgive as the Lord forgave you.

Colossians 3:13

Be kind and compassionate to one another, forgiving each other, just as in Christ God forgave you.

Ephesians 4:32

But You are a forgiving God, gracious and compassionate, slow to anger and abounding in love.

Nehemiah 9:17

If You, O LORD, kept a record of sins, O LORD, who could stand? But with You there is forgiveness; therefore You are feared.

Psalm 130:3-4

Prophets testify about Him that everyone who believes in Him receives forgiveness of sins through His name.

Acts 10:43

If we confess our sins, He is faithful and just and will forgive us our sins and purify us from all unrighteousness.

I John 1:9

"For if you forgive men when they sin against you, your heavenly Father will also forgive you. But if you do not forgive men their sins, your Father will not forgive your sins."

Matthew 6:14-15

Then I acknowledged my sin to You and did not cover up my iniquity. I said, "I will confess my transgressions to the LORD" – and You forgave the guilt of my sin.

Psalm 32:5

He who cannot forgive
breaks the bridge over which
he himself must cross.

George Herbert

❧

Dear Father, I'm so thankful for Your forgiveness, probably because I need it so often. Help me to learn from my mistakes and not have to continually ask forgiveness for the same things. Thank You for Your patience and love.

Amen.

The Blessing of Christ

Do you realize how much God loves you? Don't just blow off that question. Stop and think about it. God loves YOU.

There is indisputable evidence of His love in the Person of Jesus Christ. The illustration is often used that Christ's life can be viewed as a bridge. His life, death and resurrection make it possible for you to have a personal relationship with God. He bridged the gap between your sinfulness and God's perfection. Walking across the bridge of Christ's sacrifice cleanses you and allows you to be in God's presence.

What a blessing the gift of Christ is to each of us. Without His sacrifice we could not have a personal relationship with God. When you begin counting your blessings, the gift of Christ coming to earth will undoubtedly be at the top because it changed everything in this world.

The possibility of a relationship with God, all it offers, and the promise of heaven are available because of the blessing of Christ coming to earth. That's the number one blessing!

"For God so loved the world that He gave His one and only Son, that whoever believes in Him shall not perish but have eternal life."

John 3:16

But God demonstrates His own love for us in this: While we were still sinners, Christ died for us.

Romans 5:8

For Christ died for sins once for all, the righteous for the unrighteous, to bring you to God.

I Peter 3:18

For to me, to live is Christ and to die is gain.

Philippians 1:21

We were therefore buried with Him through baptism into death in order that, just as Christ was raised from the dead through the glory of the Father, we too may live a new life.

Romans 6:4

Jesus Christ is the same yesterday and today and forever.

Hebrews 13:8

Righteousness from God comes through faith in Jesus Christ to all who believe.

Romans 3:22

This is how we know what love is: Jesus Christ laid down His life for us. And we ought to lay down our lives for our brothers.

1 John 3:16

Being a Christian is more than just an instantaneous conversion – it is a daily process whereby you grow more and more to be like Christ.

Billy Graham

❧

Dear Father, yes, that's what I want. I want to be more and more like Christ in my thoughts, words and actions. Teach me how, Father, teach me how.

Amen.

The Blessing of Someone Listening

"I just want someone to listen to me. I wish someone would care enough to hear what I'm feeling and what I think." Have you ever felt that way?

Being listened to validates you as a person. It is evidence that someone cares enough about you to want to know what you're going through. It shows that you matter to someone. Everyone needs to know that they matter; that their presence on this earth makes a difference to others.

Think about how good it makes you feel when someone listens as you talk about your feelings, problems or joys. It connects you to your listening friend. You can also do the same for your friends – listen as they talk about their lives and families. Really hear as they discuss hopes, fears and dreams. Listening to them shows them that you care and that you are willing to invest your time and emotion into them.

What a blessing it is to be heard and to be able to listen to others.

My dear brothers, take note of this: Everyone should be quick to listen, slow to speak and slow to become angry.

James 1:19

"Love your neighbor as yourself."

Leviticus 19:18

Seek justice, encourage the oppressed.

Isaiah 1:17

We have different gifts, according to the grace given us ... If it is serving, let him serve; if it is teaching, let him teach; if it is encouraging, let him encourage.

Romans 12:6-8

Be devoted to one another in brotherly love. Honor one another above yourselves.

Romans 12:10

Above all, love each other deeply, because love covers over a multitude of sins.

1 Peter 4:8

Let us consider how we may spur one another on toward love and good deeds.

Hebrews 10:24

Be completely humble and gentle; be patient, bearing with one another in love.

Ephesians 4:2

Everyone hears what you say.
Friends listen to what you say.
Best friends listen to what you don't say.
Anonymous

❧

Dear Father, thank You for the people in my life who listen to me. It means so much to have someone listen to what I say ... and what I can't say. Thank You for people who care enough to listen that way.

Amen.

The Blessing of Hearing of God's Work

What holds your beliefs strong in those times when God seems to be silent? One encouragement to hold onto is hearing stories about God's work in the lives of His people.

Hearing of God's provision in another's life encourages you to know that He will also provide for your needs. When you hear of His protection surrounding someone then you remember that He will similarly protect you and those you love. Stories of God working by guiding and directing His children's lives is a reminder that God is alive and well, even if you can't really sense His hand on your life at the moment.

When you are discouraged, Satan will try to convince you that God has stopped working – that He doesn't care what happens in your life. Satan is pretty sneaky that way. Reading stories of God's amazing work or hearing someone tell their story is an encouragement to hang on, keep trusting and believe with all your heart that God is also working on your behalf.

Though an army besiege me, my heart will not fear; though war break out against me, even then will I be confident.

Psalm 27:3

Then the LORD said to Moses, "I will rain down bread from heaven for you."

Exodus 16:4

When Jesus saw their faith, He said, "Friend, your sins are forgiven."

Luke 5:20

"No good tree bears bad fruit, nor does a bad tree bear good fruit. Each tree is recognized by its own fruit."

Luke 6:43-44

Those who are wise will shine like the brightness of the heavens, and those who lead many to righteousness, like the stars for ever and ever.

Daniel 12:3

Jesus heard that they had thrown him out, and when He found him, He said, "Do you believe in the Son of Man?" "Who is He, Sir?" the man asked. "Tell me so that I may believe in Him." Jesus said, "You have now seen Him; in fact, He is the one speaking with you." Then the man said, "Lord, I believe," and he worshiped Him.

John 9:35-38

We are therefore Christ's ambassadors, as though God were making His appeal through us.

2 Corinthians 5:20

Then I heard the voice of the LORD saying, "Whom shall I send? And who will go for us?" And I said, "Here am I. Send me!"

Isaiah 6:8

"Come, follow Me," Jesus said, "and I will make you fishers of men."

Mark 1:17

*The discipline of gratitude is the
explicit effort to acknowledge that all I
am and have is given to me as a gift
of love, a gift to be celebrated with joy.*

Henri Nouwen

✑

Dear Father, all I am and all I have is because of You. Thank You for stories that encourage me to remember Your strength, love
and power. Help me to share my stories with
others.

Amen.

The Blessing of Peace

Life gets crazier and crazier as our planet gets more crowded; busyness takes over our days and those we care about have problems and needs.

It's a challenge to find a moment's peace in your life. Actually, it is a choice rather than a challenge. You can have a personal relationship with God who loves you more than you can even imagine, so the peace He offers is available to you. How do you access this peace? That's where the choice comes in.

You must choose to trust God with your problems and fears. To be successful at this, it is necessary to set aside time in your day to be still – be quiet before Him. That's the time when you will hear His voice, sense that He will lift the weights from your shoulders and carry your problems and fears for you.

Peace that is at rest in your soul, calmness in your heart, trust that radiates through your very being comes from your relationship with the One who loves you so much.

I will lie down and sleep in peace, for You alone, O LORD, make me dwell in safety.

Psalm 4:8

"Be still, and know that I am God; I will be exalted among the nations, I will be exalted in the earth."

Psalm 46:10

The peace of God, which transcends all understanding, will guard your hearts and your minds in Christ Jesus.

Philippians 4:7

"Come to Me, all you who are weary and burdened, and I will give you rest. Take My yoke upon you and learn from Me, for I am gentle and humble in heart, and you will find rest for your souls."

Matthew 11:28-29

"Fear not, for I have redeemed you; I have summoned you by name; you are Mine. When you pass through the waters, I will be with you; and when you pass through the rivers, they will not sweep over you."

Isaiah 43:1-2

Now may the Lord of peace Himself give you peace at all times and in every way. The Lord be with all of you.

2 Thessalonians 3:16

You will keep in perfect peace him whose mind is steadfast, because he trusts in You.

Isaiah 26:3

Let the peace of Christ rule in your hearts, since as members of one body you were called to peace. And be thankful.

Colossians 3:15

*Peace is the deliberate adjustment
of my life to the will of God.*
                              Anonymous

❧

*Dear Father, how I long for peace in my life. I
yearn for stillness and quiet times. I want the
peacefulness of knowing ... believing that You
are in control. Increase my faith so that I may
rest in You.*

                              Amen.

The Blessing of Creation

From majestic snow-capped mountains to flatland plains that stretch out forever. From the crashing of ocean waves to gentle babbling brooks. The beautiful world we live in is a gift from the Creator Himself.

Some find great joy in the raging beauty of a fiery sunset. Some feel peace from viewing a delicate rose. What a creative God we have! He knew that different people would find joy in different forms of nature and He made something for everyone.

Just look around at the creativity and diversity of nature. Compare the tiny hummingbird to the massive humpback whale. See the intricacies of a leaf and the complexities of stalagmites and stalactites in a cave.

Creation is truly amazing. It's a reminder of the power and ability of God. There is nothing too big for Him to handle or too complicated for His abilities. Nothing. Creation proves it.

For by Him all things were created: things in heaven and on earth, visible and invisible, whether thrones or powers or rulers or authorities; all things were created by Him and for Him.

Colossians 1:16

He has made everything beautiful in its time. He has also set eternity in the hearts of men; yet they cannot fathom what God has done from beginning to end.

Ecclesiastes 3:11

In the beginning You laid the foundations of the earth, and the heavens are the work of Your hands. They will perish, but You remain; they will all wear out like a garment. Like clothing You will change them and they will be discarded. But You remain the same, and Your years will never end.

Psalm 102:25-27

For You created my inmost being; You knit me together in my mother's womb. I praise You because I am fearfully and wonderfully made; Your works are wonderful, I know that full well.

Psalm 139:13-14

Through Him all things were made; without Him nothing was made that has been made.

John 1:3

The LORD, your Redeemer and Creator, says: "I am the LORD who made all things. I alone stretched out the heavens. By Myself I made the earth and everything in it.

Isaiah 44:24 NLT

O Israel, how can you say the LORD does not see your troubles? How can you say God refuses to hear your case? Don't you know that the LORD is the everlasting God, the Creator of all the earth? He never grows faint or weary. No one can measure the depths of His understanding.

Isaiah 40:27-28 NLT

Yet, O LORD, You are our Father. We are the clay, You are the potter; we are all the work of Your hand.

Isaiah 64:8

Those who contemplate the beauty of the earth find reserves of strength that will endure as long as life lasts.

Rachel Carson

❧

Dear Father, I am constantly amazed at the beauty of this world. You made something for everyone to enjoy. I love the power and beauty of the oceans and the glory of the majestic mountains. Our world shows Your creativity and power. Thank You for all You've made.

Amen.

The Blessing of Giving

You've probably heard the saying, "It's more blessed to give than to receive." Children who are reprimanded with this saying (usually when they are complaining about something they didn't get) don't seem to understand the concept. That's because it is evidence of maturity when you begin to understand this truth. When you give to someone and can appreciate the joy your gift brings then the truth of this saying begins to make sense.

It is wonderful to be the recipient of gifts or of another person's time. It helps you know you are special and loved. So, the opportunity to be the reason someone else feels that joy is wonderful. It connects you to another person when you give in order to make their life better. Jesus said that real love is shown when a person lays down his life for a friend – that's the ultimate in giving.

Does laying down your life mean dying for another person? Not necessarily, it could mean giving your time, energy, emotions and creativity to enhance another's life. What a joy to be able to do that.

"Freely you have received, freely give."

Matthew 10:8

"Give, and it will be given to you. A good measure, pressed down, shaken together and running over, will be poured into your lap."

Luke 6:38

In everything I did, I showed you that by this kind of hard work we must help the weak, remembering the words the Lord Jesus Himself said: "It is more blessed to give than to receive."

Acts 20:35

Each man should give what he has decided in his heart to give, not reluctantly or under compulsion, for God loves a cheerful giver.

2 Corinthians 9:7

Just as you excel in everything – in faith, in speech, in knowledge, in complete earnestness and in your love for us – see that you also excel in this grace of giving.

2 Corinthians 8:7

"Greater love has no one than this, that he lay down his life for his friends."

John 15:13

"When you give to the needy, do not let your left hand know what your right hand is doing, so that your giving may be in secret. Then your Father, who sees what is done in secret, will reward you."

Matthew 6:3-4

A gift opens the way for the giver and ushers him into the presence of the great.

Proverbs 18:16

The Lord loveth a cheerful giver.
He also accepteth from a grouch.

Anonymous

❧

Dear Father, when I stop and think about all that is given to me every day, I'm humbled with gratitude. Other people are so kind to me, but even their amazing kindness is over-shadowed by all You give me ... every single day. I am so grateful!

Amen.

The Blessing of Strength

Strength is an important character quality. However, most women don't want to be known for their rippling muscles, flexed to iron firmness – not that most women work to achieve that physical condition.

However, there are other kinds of strength besides physical strength. An old movie called *Steel Magnolias* honored the power of the inner strength that can be found in women. Emotional strength carries you through painful losses and relationship difficulties. Spiritual strength draws you closer to God, helping you withstand temptations and doubts.

Of course, the actual source of all strength is God. He is the iron rod that will hold you up; keep you going when you think you can't take another step; move you forward when you can't see the path. He loves you, and because of that love He promises never to leave you; promises to walk with you through whatever life brings. He promises to be your strength when you haven't got the strength to lift your head or hand.

The name of the LORD is a strong tower; the righteous run to it and are safe.

Proverbs 18:10

"I will strengthen you and help you; I will uphold you with My righteous right hand."

Isaiah 41:10

For You have been my refuge, a strong tower against the foe.

Psalm 61:3

Those who hope in the LORD will renew their strength. They will soar on wings like eagles; they will run and not grow weary, they will walk and not be faint.

Isaiah 40:31

Do not grieve, for the joy of the LORD is your strength.

Nehemiah 8:10

Be strong in the Lord and in His mighty power.

Ephesians 6:10

I can do everything through Him who gives me strength.

Philippians 4:13

The Lord stood at my side and gave me strength, so that through me the message might be fully proclaimed and all the Gentiles might hear it.

2 Timothy 4:17

No trouble can come so near
that God is not nearer.

Anonymous

❧

Dear Father, thank You for being my strength, for guiding me through life's difficulties and for never leaving me alone. I know that I can do anything because You are with me.

Amen.

The Blessing of Memories

Close your eyes and let your memory float back to the far corners of your mind. Remember birthday parties, family vacations, pizza and game nights, baking cookies with Grandma, fishing with Dad, shopping with Mom, sleepovers with girlfriends.

Every person has memories that connect them to their past and to people who have played a part in their lives.

What a joy it is to remember those who have loved you, taught you and invested in your life. Memories give you a history. They give you marking points of times of growth in your life. Memories remind you of difficult times you've made it through, and encourage you to keep on going in hard times.

Looking back through your memories shows you the thread of God's guidance, direction and protection in your life. Memories remind you that you are not alone in this world.

Love the LORD your God with all your heart and with all your soul and with all your strength. These commandments that I give you today are to be upon your hearts. Impress them on your children. Talk about them when you sit at home and when you walk along the road, when you lie down and when you get up. Tie them as symbols on your hands and bind them on your foreheads. Write them on the doorframes of your houses and on your gates.

Deuteronomy 6:5-9

Remember the wonders He has done, His miracles, and the judgments He pronounced, O descendants of Israel His servant, O sons of Jacob, His chosen ones.

1 Chronicles 16:12-13

You hear, O LORD, the desire of the afflicted; You encourage them, and You listen to their cry, defending the fatherless and the oppressed, in order that man, who is of the earth, may terrify no more.

Psalm 10:17-18

Teach me Your way, O Lord, and I will walk in Your truth; give me an undivided heart that I may fear Your name.

Psalm 86:11

For the Lord God is a sun and shield; the Lord bestows favor and honor; no good thing does He withhold from those whose walk is blameless.

Psalm 84:11

This is how God showed His love among us: He sent His one and only Son into the world that we might live through Him.

1 John 4:9

I pray that you, being rooted and established in love, may have power, together with all the saints, to grasp how wide and long and high and deep is the love of Christ, and to know this love that surpasses knowledge – that you may be filled to the measure of all the fullness of God.

Ephesians 3:17-19

God gave us memory that we might have roses in December.
James M. Barrie

❧

Dear Father, the older I get the more important my memories are to me. Thank You for all the people who have played an important role in my life.

Thank You for experiences I've learned from, even the hard ones. Thank You for giving me such great memories to draw on.

Amen.

The Blessing of Second Chances

You've just blown it ... again. Lost your temper, said the wrong thing, blown your diet, went back to an old habit or hurt someone you love. Whatever it is, are you wondering if this is the time when it's all over?

Is this the time when your loved one walks away or your boss tells you to pack up and leave? Is this the time you give up and eat the entire bag of cookies? Is this time the last time?

Thank God for the blessing of second chances. Sure, sometimes people will walk away from you – tired of the same hurts or broken promises. But sometimes those people will give you one more chance to get it right, one more chance to correct the problems.

But what's most wonderful is that God never gives up on you. He constantly gives you one more chance. He looks at your heart's desire and gives you chance after chance to obey more, love more and learn more. Thank God for second chances.

From inside the fish Jonah prayed to the LORD his God ... Then the word of the LORD came to Jonah a second time: "Go to the great city of Nineveh and proclaim to it the message I give you."

Jonah 2:1; 3:1-2

Godly sorrow brings repentance that leads to salvation and leaves no regret, but worldly sorrow brings death.

2 Corinthians 7:10

Therefore this is what the LORD says: "If you repent, I will restore you that you may serve Me; if you utter worthy, not worthless, words, you will be My spokesman."

Jeremiah 15:19

This is love for God: to obey His commands.

1 John 5:3

We know that we have passed from death to life, because we love our brothers. Anyone who does not love remains in death.

1 John 3:14

No, in all these things we are more than conquerors through Him who loved us. For I am convinced that neither death nor life, neither angels nor demons, neither the present nor the future, nor any powers, neither height nor depth, nor anything else in all creation, will be able to separate us from the love of God that is in Christ Jesus our Lord.

Romans 8:37-39

If I speak in the tongues of men and of angels, but have not love, I am only a resounding gong or a clanging cymbal.

1 Corinthians 13:1

For everything that was written in the past was written to teach us, so that through endurance and the encouragement of the Scriptures we might have hope.

Romans 15:4

To fear is to expect punishment.
To love is to know we are immersed
not in darkness but in light.

Mother Teresa

❧

Dear Father, thank You for not giving up on
me. Thank You for love that keeps getting me
back on my feet to try and try again. It's only
because of You giving me second chances
that I have the strength to keep trying to be
the woman You believe I can be.

Amen.

The Blessing of Salvation

He didn't have to do it. God did not *have* to send Jesus to earth. He didn't *have* to sacrifice His Son. Jesus didn't *have* to leave heaven and endure the persecution, ridicule, suffering and finally, murder that He was subjected to on this earth. He didn't have to – so why did He? Because He loves you. That's the bottom line.

God loves you so much that He wanted to make a way for you to be with Him forever. Salvation. God's love provided a way for you to be forgiven of all your sin; a way for you to have a personal relationship with Him; a way for you to enter His perfect heaven and be with Him forever.

This gift of love was not free to Him. Your salvation came at a cost to Him, but is free to you because of love. Simply put, God loves you.

"For God so loved the world that He gave His one and only Son, that whoever believes in Him shall not perish but have eternal life."

John 3:16

Because of His great love for us, God, who is rich in mercy, made us alive with Christ even when we were dead in transgressions.

Ephesians 2:4-5

This is how God showed His love among us: He sent His one and only Son into the world that we might live through Him. This is love: not that we loved God, but that He loved us and sent His Son as an atoning sacrifice for our sins.

1 John 4:9-10

For to us a Child is born, to us a Son is given, and the government will be on His shoulders. And He will be called Wonderful Counselor, Mighty God, Everlasting Father, Prince of Peace.

Isaiah 9:6

Therefore, there is now no condemnation for those who are in Christ Jesus, because through Christ Jesus the law of the Spirit of life set me free from the law of sin and death.

Romans 8:1-2

The Lord is my light and my salvation – whom shall I fear?

Psalm 27:1

Salvation is found in no one else, for there is no other name under heaven given to men by which we must be saved.

Acts 4:12

My soul finds rest in God alone; my salvation comes from Him. He alone is my rock and my salvation; He is my fortress, I will never be shaken

Psalm 62:1-2

God proved His love on the cross.
When Christ hung, and bled,
and died, it was God saying
to the world, "I love you."
        Billy Graham

❧

Dear Father, I cannot comprehend, cannot be-
gin to understand Your love that would give
the life of Your Son for me. I am overcome
with love for You and thankfulness for the
gift of salvation. I pray to be reminded every
day of the magnitude of this gift to me.

                    Amen.

The Blessing of Family

Family – the people with whom you can most be yourself. When you come in the house and close the door, all pretenses can drop, the effort to impress is gone.

You are just you, and, for the most part, your family will love you no matter what. Of course, that's allowing for the normal growing pains of family life. Family gives you a lot more than a gene pool, family gives you a context in which to build your life.

You begin with parents who love you more than you understand (until you become a parent), siblings with whom you create imaginary worlds of play, share birthdays and Christmas memories. Siblings whom you will have in your world the rest of your life.

Family includes extended members who all play a part in your life. Living in a family unit teaches love, patience, acceptance, patience, forgiveness and patience. You get to choose your friends in life but family are given to you. Friends may come and go but family will always be there.

Sons are a heritage from the LORD, children a reward from Him.

Psalm 127:3

Train a child in the way he should go, and when he is old he will not turn from it.

Proverbs 22:6

I have been reminded of your sincere faith, which first lived in your grandmother Lois and in your mother Eunice and, I am persuaded, now lives in you also.

2 Timothy 1:5

There, in the presence of the LORD your God, you and your families shall eat and shall rejoice in everything you have put your hand to, because the LORD your God has blessed you.

Deuteronomy 12:7

Finally, all of you, live in harmony with one another; be sympathetic, love as brothers, be compassionate and humble.

1 Peter 3:8

God sets the lonely in families, He leads forth the prisoners with singing; but the rebellious live in a sun-scorched land.

Psalm 68:6

Now that you have purified yourselves by obeying the truth so that you have sincere love for your brothers, love one another deeply, from the heart.

I Peter 1:22

This is His command: to believe in the name of His Son, Jesus Christ, and to love one another as He commanded us.

I John 3:23

There are no adequate substitutes for father, mother, and children bound together in a loving commitment to nurture and protect. No government, no matter how well-intentioned, can take the place of the family in the scheme of things.

President Gerald R. Ford

❧

Dear Father, I love my family, even with all their bumps and bruises. I know they are not perfect, neither am I. But we love one another and we'll be there for each other, no matter what life brings. Thank You for them. Thank You for what each of them bring to the family.

Amen.

The Blessing of God's Word

Do you know that moment of joy when you open your e-mail and a letter pops up from someone you haven't heard from in a very long time? It's even better if the letter is long and newsy, catching you up on things going on in your friend's life. Letters refresh relationships that get foggy without connections.

The Bible is sometimes called God's letter to His children. Reading it gives a history to God's relationships and actions. You begin to understand His character by how He related to people in Bible times. You see His patience, love and, yes, His judgment, too. God's Word gives instructions and guidance. It is His message to you, His child.

Reading God's Word will help you understand Him and His plan for your life. It will teach you how to live for Him, share Him with others and become more and more like Christ.

All Scripture is God-breathed and is useful for teaching, rebuking, correcting and training in righteousness, so that the man of God may be thoroughly equipped for every good work.

2 Timothy 3:16-17

Above all, you must understand that no prophecy of Scripture came about by the prophet's own interpretation. For prophecy never had its origin in the will of man, but men spoke from God as they were carried along by the Holy Spirit.

2 Peter 1:20-21

The lamp of the LORD searches the spirit of a man; it searches out his inmost being.

Proverbs 20:27

For the word of God is living and active. Sharper than any double-edged sword, it penetrates even to dividing soul and spirit, joints and marrow; it judges the thoughts and attitudes of the heart.

Hebrews 4:12

Your word is a lamp to my feet and a light for my path.

Psalm 119:105

He humbled you, causing you to hunger and then feeding you with manna, which neither you nor your fathers had known, to teach you that man does not live on bread alone but on every word that comes from the mouth of the LORD.

Deuteronomy 8:3

These commandments that I give you today are to be upon your hearts. Impress them on your children. Talk about them when you sit at home and when you walk along the road, when you lie down and when you get up. Tie them as symbols on your hands and bind them on your foreheads. Write them on the doorframes of your houses and on your gates.

Deuteronomy 6:6-9

It is not enough to own a Bible;
we must read it. It is not enough
to read it; we must let it speak to us.
It is not enough to let it speak to us;
we must believe it. It is not enough
to believe it; we must live it.

William A. Ward

❧

Dear Father, Your Word speaks to me every time I read it. There is hope and power in it. Thank You for giving me the Bible so that I may get to know You and Your love.

Amen.

The Blessing of God's Character

There aren't many things in this life that you can count on always being there and always being the same. What can you think of that is constant, sure and steady?

People come and go, their loyalty and love ebbs and flows, jobs disappear, situations change. That's the word – change – it's a constant in life. The one thing you can always count on is God.

He is always present and always the same. His character is steady. It is not dependent on moods or situations. You know Him through His Word and through your past experiences with Him so you know His character.

Unlike a human, He will never act contrary to who He is. He always has your best interests in mind – even when that means allowing you to learn from mistakes or painful situations.

What a comfort to know that God is. His character is an anchor to hang everything else in life on because it is steady and sure and defined by love.

Jesus Christ is the same yesterday and today and forever.

Hebrews 13:8

He who is the Glory of Israel does not lie or change His mind; for He is not a man, that He should change His mind.

1 Samuel 15:29

God is not a man, that He should lie, nor a son of man, that He should change His mind. Does He speak and then not act? Does He promise and not fulfill?

Numbers 23:19

For the LORD is good and His love endures forever; His faithfulness continues through all generations.

Psalm 100:5

"As the Father has loved Me, so have I loved you. Now remain in My love."

John 15:9

One thing God has spoken, two things have I heard: that You, O God, are strong, and that You, O LORD, are loving. Surely You will reward each person according to what he has done.

Psalm 62:11-12

Who shall separate us from the love of Christ? Shall trouble or hardship or persecution or famine or nakedness or danger or sword?

Romans 8:35

For He chose us in Him before the creation of the world to be holy and blameless in His sight. In love He predestined us to be adopted as His sons through Jesus Christ, in accordance with His pleasure and will – to the praise of His glorious grace, which He has freely given us in the One He loves.

Ephesians 1:4-6

Nothing can alter the character of God. In the course of a human life, tastes and outlook and temper may change radically: a kind, equable man may turn bitter and crotchety: a man of good-will may grow cynical and callous. But nothing of this sort happens to the Creator. He never becomes less truthful, or merciful, or just, or good, than He used to be.

J. I. Packer

❧

Dear Father, I'm so thankful that You never change. Your character is the one thing in this world that I can count on always being the same. You are dependable, constant and the very definition of love. Thank You for that.

Amen.

The Blessing of Discipline

Discipline is a blessing? Maybe that's a hard concept for you. After all, no one enjoys being disciplined. Just the word brings up memories of being confined to your room or being grounded – in short, punishment, without always understanding why the discipline was being meted out.

To be sure, sometimes human discipline is more punishment than true discipline and is based on the mood of another person.

It's important to remember that when God disciplines you there is a reason. It is never the result of His tiredness or irritability. God's discipline helps you learn to obey Him more and walk closer with Him. God's discipline is intended to help you grow into all the possibilities He sees for you.

While it is sometimes painful and unpleasant, God's discipline is a blessing because it moves you forward in the process of becoming more like Christ.

Know then in your heart that as a man disciplines his son, so the LORD your God disciplines you.

Deuteronomy 8:5

Endure hardship as discipline; God is treating you as sons. For what son is not disciplined by his father? If you are not disciplined (and everyone undergoes discipline), then you are illegitimate children and not true sons.

Hebrews 12:7-8

Our fathers disciplined us for a little while as they thought best; but God disciplines us for our good, that we may share in His holiness. No discipline seems pleasant at the time, but painful. Later on, however, it produces a harvest of righteousness and peace for those who have been trained by it.

Hebrews 12:10-11

Blessed is the man You discipline, O LORD, the man You teach from Your law.

Psalm 94:12

Whoever loves discipline loves knowledge, but he who hates correction is stupid.

Proverbs 12:1

My son, do not despise the LORD's discipline and do not resent His rebuke, because the LORD disciplines those He loves, as a father the son he delights in.

Proverbs 3:11-12

Blessed is the man whom God corrects; so do not despise the discipline of the Almighty.

Job 5:17

When we ask God to do something for us, He generally wants to do something in us.

Anonymous

❧

Dear Father, I am not fond of discipline. It hurts. Help me to face discipline with the understanding that it is helping me grow into a better person and a stronger Christian. Give me the wisdom to learn from it and then to move forward.

Amen.

The Blessing of Eternal Life

Teenagers seem to think that they will live forever. Life is exciting and they love taking chances that make their parents' hearts quiver. Kids can't imagine anything serious happening to them.

But teenagers grow up and as people mature, they gradually gain the understanding that life doesn't last forever. Maturity brings an appreciation that there is definitely an eternity and that everyone will spend their eternity somewhere.

Think for a moment of options that present themselves, then stand up and shout, "Thank God for salvation!" The gift of Jesus – His death and resurrection – makes it possible for you to have the assurance of eternal life in heaven with God.

There would be no other way. Eternity in heaven promises being in God's presence, joy, happiness and an eternity filled with love. This blessing is yours when you accept Jesus as your Savior. God promised it.

"If anyone would come after Me, he must deny himself and take up his cross and follow Me. For whoever wants to save his life will lose it, but whoever loses his life for Me will find it."

Matthew 16:24-25

"The man who loves his life will lose it, while the man who hates his life in this world will keep it for eternal life."

John 12:25

For the wages of sin is death, but the gift of God is eternal life in Christ Jesus our Lord.

Romans 6:23

"Do not let your hearts be troubled. Trust in God; trust also in Me. In My Father's house are many rooms; if it were not so, I would have told you. I am going there to prepare a place for you. And if I go and prepare a place for you, I will come back and take you to be with Me that you also may be where I am."

John 14:1-3

"He who overcomes will, like them, be dressed in white. I will never blot out his name from the book of life, but will acknowledge his name before My Father and His angels."

Revelation 3:5

"Seek first His kingdom and His righteousness, and all these things will be given to you as well."

Matthew 6:33

"Store up for yourselves treasures in heaven, where moth and rust do not destroy, and where thieves do not break in and steal. For where your treasure is, there your heart will be also."

Matthew 6:20-21

Since, then, you have been raised with Christ, set your hearts on things above, where Christ is seated at the right hand of God.

Colossians 3:1

I'm not going to heaven because I've preached to great crowds of people. I'm going to heaven because Christ died on that cross. None of us are going to heaven because we're good. And we're not going to heaven because we've worked. We're not going to heaven because we pray and accept Christ. We're going to heaven because of what He did on the Cross. All I have to do is receive Him. And it's so easy to receive Christ that millions stumble over its sheer simplicity.

Billy Graham

❧

Dear Father, thank You for salvation. It is truly a gift of love. Help me to understand the urgency of sharing the message of salvation. Give me a heart to reach the world with the message of salvation.

Amen.

The Blessing of Met Needs

When you have a problem it is definitely a blessing to have someone listen as you talk it through. But an even greater blessing occurs when someone goes out of their way to actually meet your needs in any way they can.

When another person invests his or her time and energy into your life, it makes you feel special and loved, especially if that person must make an effort to help you. Kind words are fine. Prayer is wonderful. But when something could actually be done to meet your needs, words are rather empty. There is also the possibility that a friend's actions could actually be the answer to his or her own prayer on your behalf. Having your needs met is definitely a blessing.

Of course, the greatest "Need-Meeter" is God. When you cry out He will meet your needs, sometimes immediately, sometimes in His own time. There are times when you only become aware of His work in your life as you look back. Knowing that God cares for you enough to meet your needs brings a peaceful comfort.

Cast all your anxiety on Him because He cares for you.

I Peter 5:7

Delight yourself in the LORD and He will give you the desires of your heart.

Psalm 37:4

"Therefore I tell you, do not worry about your life, what you will eat or drink; or about your body, what you will wear ... If that is how God clothes the grass of the field, which is here today and tomorrow is thrown into the fire, will He not much more clothe you, O you of little faith?"

Matthew 6:25, 30

Cast your cares on the LORD and He will sustain you; He will never let the righteous fall.

Psalm 55:22

The LORD is good, a refuge in times of trouble. He cares for those who trust in Him.

Nahum 1:7

"So do not fear, for I am with you; do not be dismayed, for I am your God. I will strengthen you and help you; I will uphold you with My righteous right hand."

Isaiah 41:10

Therefore we do not lose heart. Though outwardly we are wasting away, yet inwardly we are being renewed day by day.

2 Corinthians 4:16

Because of the LORD's great love we are not consumed, for His compassions never fail. They are new every morning; great is Your faithfulness.

Lamentations 3:22-23

God is even kinder than you think.

St. Theresa

❧

Dear Father, that quotation gives me something to think about. You are kind because You love me. But that love is so incredible that I can't begin to comprehend it.

Thank You for loving me. Thank You for meeting even the smallest of my needs. You are amazing.

Amen.

The Blessing of the Holy Spirit

God is Trinity – three distinct Persons, yet one God. God the Father, Jesus the Son and the Holy Spirit. The Holy Spirit is probably the most misunderstood part of the Trinity.

We know that Jesus came to earth, lived and taught, was murdered, then rose from the dead. Before He returned to heaven, He promised to send the Holy Spirit – God's presence to dwell in believers.

The Holy Spirit is the warmth of God's presence. He gives guidance and direction by speaking into the believer's heart and mind. The Holy Spirit is God in you. This presence of God inside you guides your thoughts, challenges your heart to turn to God, fills you with the sense of God's love.

He prays for you when your heart is so distraught that you can't find words to speak. He is God and He is your connection to God.

Where can I go from Your Spirit? Where can I flee from Your presence?

Psalm 139:7

"Therefore go and make disciples of all nations, baptizing them in the name of the Father and of the Son and of the Holy Spirit, and teaching them to obey everything I have commanded you."

Matthew 28:19-20

"The Counselor, the Holy Spirit, whom the Father will send in My name, will teach you all things and will remind you of everything I have said to you."

John 14:26

So I say, live by the Spirit, and you will not gratify the desires of the sinful nature.

Galatians 5:16

The fruit of the Spirit is love, joy, peace, patience, kindness, goodness, faithfulness, gentleness and self-control

Galatians 5:22-23

In the same way, the Spirit helps us in our weakness. We do not know what we ought to pray for, but the Spirit Himself intercedes for us with groans that words cannot express.

Romans 8:26

Since we live by the Spirit, let us keep in step with the Spirit.

Galatians 5:25

It is God who has made us for this very purpose and has given us the Spirit as a deposit, guaranteeing what is to come.

2 Corinthians 5:5

Trying to do the Lord's work in your own strength is the most confusing, exhausting and tedious of all work. But when you are filled with the Holy Spirit, then the ministry of Jesus just flows out of you.

Corrie Ten Boom

❧

Dear Father, thank You for the Holy Spirit's presence within me. Father, help me learn how to live in His power, allowing it to guide and direct me and to flow through me.

Amen.

The Blessing of a History with God

New relationships are fun. You're learning things about each other and it's exciting. The difficult part about a new relationship is that you don't know each other so you don't know what kind of actions or reactions to expect.

You don't know what kind of emotions a given set of experiences or situations will set off. Most importantly, you don't know if you can count on this person to be there for you in good times and bad, or if he or she is going to be more of an acquaintance than a friend. There is no history to draw on with a new friend so there is no way to know these kinds of things.

Having a history with God; being able to recall how He has worked in your life; how He has guided and directed you and how He has shown you His love, gives the comfort of knowing what to expect in your present and future relationship with Him. He has already proven His love for you, so you know you can trust Him.

Let love and faithfulness never leave you; bind them around your neck, write them on the tablet of your heart.

Proverbs 3:3

We know that in all things God works for the good of those who love Him, who have been called according to His purpose.

Romans 8:28

I urge you to live a life worthy of the calling you have received.

Ephesians 4:1

Not that I have already obtained all this, or have already been made perfect, but I press on to take hold of that for which Christ Jesus took hold of me.

Philippians 3:12

Speaking the truth in love, we will in all things grow up into Him who is the Head, that is, Christ.

Ephesians 4:15

We have heard of your faith in Christ Jesus and of the love you have for all the saints – the faith and love that spring from the hope that is stored up for you in heaven and that you have already heard about in the word of truth, the gospel that has come to you.

Colossians 1:4-6

Therefore, as God's chosen people, holy and dearly loved, clothe yourselves with compassion, kindness, humility, gentleness and patience.

Colossians 3:12

For there is one God and one mediator between God and men, the man Christ Jesus, who gave Himself as a ransom for all men.

1 Timothy 2:5-6

What I believe about God is the most important thing about me.

A. W. Tozer

❦

Dear Father, my history with You shows. What I believe about You is evident by how I live my life. Father, I pray for a daily memory of how You have worked in my life and shown Your love to me. Father, I pray for my life to show that I love and trust You.

Amen.

The Blessing of Faith

Faith is the anchor that holds your beliefs steady. Without faith your Christian walk is meaningless, prayer is pointless and your relationship with God has no foundation.

Faith is the verb that gives action to all those things. Because of faith that God is who He says He is and that His Word is alive and real, you seek to know Him more, to grow deeper in your relationship with Him.

Because of faith, you pray to God, believing with all your heart that He hears your prayers and will answer you. Because of faith you believe there is a heaven and a hell and that your choice to believe in God and accept Jesus as Savior determines which of those places will be your eternal home.

Faith is a gift from God that may start small in your heart, but as you exercise that faith it grows and grows so that, by faith you can be healed, by faith you can move mountains, by faith you can know God.

This is the victory that has overcome the world, even our faith.

I John 5:4

If I have a faith that can move mountains, but have not love, I am nothing.

I Corinthians 13:2

We live by faith, not by sight.

2 Corinthians 5:7

For it is by grace you have been saved, through faith – and this not from yourselves, it is the gift of God – not by works, so that no one can boast.

Ephesians 2:8-9

I pray that you may be active in sharing your faith, so that you will have a full understanding of every good thing we have in Christ.

Philemon 6

Faith comes from hearing the message, and the message is heard through the word of Christ.

Romans 10:17

Therefore, since we have been justified through faith, we have peace with God through our Lord Jesus Christ, through whom we have gained access by faith into this grace in which we now stand. And we rejoice in the hope of the glory of God.

Romans 5:1-2

Faith is being sure of what we hope for and certain of what we do not see.

Hebrews 11:1

Never doubt in the dark what
God told you in the light.

V. Raymond Edmund

❧

Dear Father, give me more faith. Help me to trust You in the darkest of times and in the best of times. Grow my faith to the point where You are all that matters.

Amen.

The Blessing of Love

There is no greater feeling in the world than knowing with absolute certainty that you are loved. Confidence in love gives you freedom to be yourself. You trust the person who loves you to sift through the garbage of your moods or self-centeredness, and just keep on loving you – as you do for him or her.

The one who loves you desires to help and encourage you to be the best person you can be and helps you realize your potential. Knowing you are loved is like living inside a high, protective security fence and at the same time having complete and total freedom. Love brings happiness, joy, security and fulfillment.

Of course, the ultimate love experience is with God. We love because He first loved us. It all began there. God's love for you is full and complete. It is unconditional and beyond understanding. God's love surrounds you and lifts you up from your own weak self-image and disappointments. Love, both human and divine is the ultimate blessing.

"A new command I give you: Love one another. As I have loved you, so you must love one another. By this all men will know that you are My disciples, if you love one another."

John 13:34-35

Jesus replied: "'Love the Lord your God with all your heart and with all your soul and with all your mind.' This is the first and greatest commandment. And the second is like it: 'Love your neighbor as yourself.'"

Matthew 22:37-39

Love is patient, love is kind. It does not envy, it does not boast, it is not proud. It is not rude, it is not self-seeking, it is not easily angered, it keeps no record of wrongs. Love does not delight in evil but rejoices with the truth. It always protects, always trusts, always hopes, always perseveres.

I Corinthians 13:4-7

I will sing of the LORD's great love forever; with my mouth I will make Your faithfulness known through all generations.

Psalm 89:1

The LORD, the LORD, the compassionate and gracious God, slow to anger, abounding in love and faithfulness, maintaining love to thousands, and forgiving wickedness, rebellion and sin.

Exodus 34:6-7

"I have loved you with an everlasting love; I have drawn you with loving-kindness."

Jeremiah 31:3

How great is the love the Father has lavished on us, that we should be called children of God! And that is what we are!

1 John 3:1

Dear friends, let us love one another, for love comes from God. Everyone who loves has been born of God and knows God. Whoever does not love does not know God, because God is love.

1 John 4:7-8

*Love is unselfishly choosing
for another's highest good.*

C. S. Lewis

❧

*Dear Father, love gives me the greatest joy. I
feel so secure and comfortable in the love of
my family and friends. Thank You for Your
love that started it all!*

Amen.

The Blessing of Laughter

How boring would life be without laughter? Even the medical community notes the importance of laughter for our physical and emotional health.

Sharing a deep, from-your-gut laugh; the kind that makes your eyes water and leaves you gasping for breath, with someone builds a great memory. It makes a marking point that the two of you can look back on. Laughter can make you forget your troubles, if only for a moment. It's a little respite in the midst of a storm.

God certainly knew how important laughter would be for us. Just think of all the things He made that bring us to that point, from the antics of kittens to the wit of gifted humorists, He gives us daily chances to shift our focus from ourselves and just enjoy one another and the wonderful world He gave us. Go ahead, laugh ... it's good for you!

There is a time for everything, and a season for every activity under heaven: a time to weep and a time to laugh.

Ecclesiastes 3:1, 4

A cheerful heart is good medicine, but a crushed spirit dries up the bones.

Proverbs 17:22

Why are you downcast, O my soul? Why so disturbed within me? Put your hope in God, for I will yet praise Him, my Savior and my God.

Psalm 43:5

Shout with joy to God, all the earth! Sing the glory of His name; make His praise glorious!

Psalm 66:1-2

I will rejoice in the LORD, I will be joyful in God my Savior.

Habakkuk 3:18

May the righteous be glad and rejoice before God; may they be happy and joyful.

Psalm 68:3

A happy heart makes the face cheerful, but heart-ache crushes the spirit.

Proverbs 15:13

Is any one of you in trouble? He should pray. Is anyone happy? Let him sing songs of praise.

James 5:13

*Laughter is the closest thing
to the grace of God.*

Karl Barth

❧

*Dear Father, laughter is real medicine to my
soul. Thank You for joyful belly laughs that I
share with my loved ones. Thank You for the
giggles and smiles. Thank You for lightening
the load of life with laughter.*

Amen.

The Blessing of Courage

You know fear. That gut-wrenching sensation that settles in your stomach, heart and mind. It controls your thoughts, motives – even your movement.

A threat to your safety, danger for your kids, life-threatening illness to a loved one and fear takes over. What do you do when that happens? Where do you find the courage to wade through fear?

The source of emotional courage is God. His Spirit dwelling in your heart is the foundation to stand on, the strength to lean on during the fearful times of life.

Courage doesn't come cheaply – you don't know you have it until you need it. But, when your heart cries out in fear and God answers with the strength to "keep on keeping on" until you have made it through the crisis, you can praise God for the blessing of courage.

Have I not commanded you? Be strong and courageous. Do not be terrified; do not be discouraged,
for the LORD your God will be with you wherever
you go.

Joshua 1:9

Be on your guard; stand firm in the faith; be men
of courage; be strong.

1 Corinthians 16:13

The LORD is my light and my salvation – whom
shall I fear? The LORD is the stronghold of my life –
of whom shall I be afraid?

Psalm 27:1

There is no fear in love. But perfect love drives out
fear, because fear has to do with punishment. The
one who fears is not made perfect in love.

1 John 4:18

I pray that out of His glorious riches He may
strengthen you with power through His Spirit in
your inner being, so that Christ may dwell in your
hearts through faith.

Ephesians 3:16-17

It is God who arms me with strength and makes my way perfect.

2 Samuel 22:33

I can do everything through Him who gives me strength.

Philippians 4:13

May our Lord Jesus Christ Himself and God our Father, who loved us and by His grace gave us eternal encouragement and good hope, encourage your hearts and strengthen you in every good deed and word.

2 Thessalonians 2:16-17

Courage is a special kind of knowledge;
the knowledge of how to fear what
ought to be feared and how not
to fear what ought not be feared.
Ben Gurion

❧

Dear Father, I'm not a very courageous person. Lots of things scare me. Thank You for Your presence with me. That makes me feel braver because I never face life alone.

Amen.

The Blessing of My Local Church

If you've ever read stories or seen movies about the brave people who settled in the American Wild West you know that the settlers traveled in wagon trains.

You may also have a visual image from movies or television shows of how they circled the wagons when they camped for protection and safety. They knew that there is safety in numbers and it's important to have a community around you.

Have you ever thought of your local church as a wagon train circle for your protection? Your church family can serve as your community; friends with whom you can share your deepest needs and grandest joys. They also, as brothers and sisters in the faith, should protect you from slipping into sinful habits by holding you accountable and challenging you to grow deeper in the faith.

When you accepted Christ you were adopted into God's family. Your local church is your personal branch of that family. Celebrate with a weekly family reunion!

Just as each of us has one body with many members, and these members do not all have the same function, so in Christ we who are many form one body, and each member belongs to all the others.

Romans 12:4-5

The body is a unit, though it is made up of many parts; and though all its parts are many, they form one body. So it is with Christ. For we were all baptized by one Spirit into one body.

I Corinthians 12:12-13

Make every effort to keep the unity of the Spirit through the bond of peace. There is one body and one Spirit – just as you were called to one hope when you were called – one Lord, one faith, one baptism; one God and Father of all, who is over all and through all and in all.

Ephesians 4:3-6

Encourage one another daily, as long as it is called Today, so that none of you may be hardened by sin's deceitfulness.

Hebrews 3:13

Let us consider how we may spur one another on toward love and good deeds. Let us not give up meeting together, as some are in the habit of doing, but let us encourage one another – and all the more as you see the Day approaching.

Hebrews 10:24-25

Be imitators of God, therefore, as dearly loved children and live a life of love, just as Christ loved us and gave Himself up for us as a fragrant offering and sacrifice to God.

Ephesians 5:1-2

Live in harmony with one another; be sympathetic, love as brothers, be compassionate and humble.

I Peter 3:8

My purpose is that they may be encouraged in heart and united in love, so that they may have the full riches of complete understanding, in order that they may know the mystery of God, namely, Christ, in whom are hidden all the treasures of wisdom and knowledge.

Colossians 2:2-3

Churchgoers are like coals in a fire.
When they cling together they
keep the flame aglow, when
they separate, they die out.

Billy Graham

Dear Father, it's so easy to criticize things at my church – the music style, the pastor, the Board members. But, when someone needs help or support, my church circles around to support them. Father, help me to be on the supporting side and not the criticizing side. Thank You for my church.

Amen.

The Blessing of God's Presence

Have you ever stopped to think how incredibly amazing it is that God, the Creator of all things, God who owns all things, God who is in control of all things – is with you *all the time*? You are never alone. Never.

Whatever you're going through, no matter how difficult or frightening, you are not alone. It's true that sometimes you may not be able to "feel" His presence, but that doesn't change the fact that He *is* with you.

He has promised to always be present. He's with you and is willing to guide and direct, to give wisdom, and to love through you. All you need to do is ask Him to do those things for you, then submit to His will and guidance.

Whatever life brings along, you can settle back and rest in His hand because He is there and nothing surprises Him. You are never alone. Always with the strength, power, wisdom and love of God available to you.

Even though I walk through the valley of the shadow of death, I will fear no evil, for You are with me; Your rod and Your staff, they comfort me.

Psalm 23:4

"Surely I am with you always, to the very end of the age."

Matthew 28:20

"You will seek Me and find Me when you seek Me with all your heart."

Jeremiah 29:13

Do not be terrified; do not be discouraged, for the LORD your God will be with you wherever you go.

Joshua 1:9

O LORD, You have searched me and You know me. You know when I sit and when I rise; You perceive my thoughts from afar. Before a word is on my tongue You know it completely, O LORD. You hem me in – behind and before; You have laid Your hand upon me.

Psalm 139:1-2; 4-5

Come near to God and He will come near to you.

James 4:8

You also were included in Christ when you heard the word of truth, the gospel of your salvation. Having believed, you were marked in Him with a seal, the promised Holy Spirit, who is a deposit guaranteeing our inheritance until the redemption of those who are God's possession – to the praise of His glory.

Ephesians 1:13-14

"I will walk among you and be your God, and you will be My people."

Leviticus 26:12

We cannot get away from God,
though we can ignore Him.

James Cabot

❧

Dear Father, Your presence is my comfort and
my strength. I know You are always with me.
Help me to always be with You.

Amen.

The Blessing of Suffering

Suffering? Really? Are you wondering if this is a misprint? It is not. Of course you don't like to suffer. What kind of fool would seek out pain?

Think about it though – how do you strengthen and tone your body's muscles to make them as effective as possible? You exercise them which takes effort and work and sometimes results in a bit of pain. The work you put your muscles through teaches them to be stronger.

Your faith grows in the same way. The more you are required to walk by faith through suffering and pain, the stronger your faith grows. So, suffering is a blessing because it helps you grow deeper in your faith, lean on God more, and trust Him to get you through difficult times.

Suffering is one of the primary ways your faith will grow stronger. So, as James says, "Consider it pure joy whenever you face trials of many kinds" (James 1:2).

In all my prayers for all of you, I always pray with joy because of your partnership in the gospel from the first day until now, being confident of this, that He who began a good work in you will carry it on to completion until the day of Christ Jesus.

Philippians 1:4-6

Consider it pure joy, my brothers, whenever you face trials of many kinds, because you know that the testing of your faith develops perseverance. Perseverance must finish its work so that you may be mature and complete, not lacking anything.

James 1:2-4

In this you greatly rejoice, though now for a little while you may have had to suffer grief in all kinds of trials. These have come so that your faith – of greater worth than gold, which perishes even though refined by fire – may be proved genuine and may result in praise, glory and honor when Jesus Christ is revealed.

1 Peter 1:6-7

For men are not cast off by the LORD forever. Though He brings grief, He will show compassion, so great is His unfailing love.

Lamentations 3:31-32

For He has not despised or disdained the suffering of the afflicted one; He has not hidden His face from him but has listened to his cry for help.

Psalm 22:24

Do your best to present yourself to God as one approved, a workman who does not need to be ashamed and who correctly handles the word of truth.

2 Timothy 2:15

Now if we are children, then we are heirs – heirs of God and co-heirs with Christ, if indeed we share in His sufferings in order that we may also share in His glory.

Romans 8:17

Suffering can become a means to greater love and greater generosity.
Mother Teresa

❧

Dear Father, I know that suffering is inevitable, but that doesn't mean I look forward to it. Please, Father, show me how to grow and learn through the sufferings of my life. Show me how to lean on You and draw closer to You.

Amen.

The Blessing of Life Itself

Life. The blessing of living and breathing on this amazing earth God created. All the other blessings would mean nothing if you weren't here to enjoy them. Recognition of the blessing of life itself leads to thankfulness for all God has given.

God, in His graciousness and mercy, allows His children to experience life – to experience loving other people, knowing His presence, love, direction and guidance. Enjoying life to the fullest is a blessing back to God.

How much pleasure He must take from hearing the joy of His children as they appreciate life and all the blessings He bestows on them. Life is a blessing. Thanking God for it blesses Him back.

I have fought the good fight, I have finished the race, I have kept the faith.

2 Timothy 4:7

The LORD your God has blessed you in all the work of your hands. He has watched over your journey through this vast desert. These forty years the LORD your God has been with you, and you have not lacked anything.

Deuteronomy 2:7

Clap your hands, all you nations; shout to God with cries of joy. How awesome is the LORD Most High, the great King over all the earth!

Psalm 47:1-2

Therefore, if anyone is in Christ, he is a new creation; the old has gone, the new has come!

2 Corinthians 5:17

Let the word of Christ dwell in you richly as you teach and admonish one another with all wisdom, and as you sing psalms, hymns and spiritual songs with gratitude in your hearts to God.

Colossians 3:16

Give thanks to the LORD, for He is good; His love endures forever.

I Chronicles 16:34

So then, just as you received Christ Jesus as Lord, continue to live in Him, rooted and built up in Him, strengthened in the faith as you were taught, and overflowing with thankfulness.

Colossians 2:6-7

Praise be to the God and Father of our Lord Jesus Christ! In His great mercy He has given us new birth into a living hope through the resurrection of Jesus Christ from the dead, and into an inheritance that can never perish, spoil or fade – kept in heaven for you, who through faith are shielded by God's power until the coming of the salvation that is ready to be revealed in the last time.

I Peter 1:3-5

The great use of life is to spend it for something that will outlast it.
William James

❧

Dear Father, I am so thankful for life. I appreciate the joy of living each day and experiencing the joy of loving and being loved.

Father, I pray that my life will count for You. Guide my thoughts and my actions into usefulness to You.

Amen.